Angelina Ballerina™

My First Ballet Class

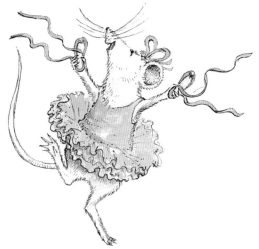

This book belongs to:

Written by **Katharine Holabird**
With illustrations by **Helen Craig**

Grosset & Dunlap

GROSSET & DUNLAP
Published by the Penguin Group
Penguin Group (USA) Inc., 375 Hudson Street,
New York, New York 10014, U.S.A.
Penguin Group (Canada), 90 Eglinton Avenue East,
Suite 700, Toronto, Ontario, Canada M4P 2Y3
(a division of Pearson Penguin Canada Inc.)
Penguin Books Ltd, 80 Strand, London WC2R 0RL, England
Penguin Ireland, 25 St Stephen's Green, Dublin 2, Ireland
(a division of Penguin Books Ltd)
Penguin Group (Australia), 250 Camberwell Road, Camberwell,
Victoria 3124, Australia (a division of Pearson Australia Group Pty Ltd)
Penguin Books India Pvt Ltd, 11 Community Centre,
Panchsheel Park, New Delhi - 110 017, India
Penguin Group (NZ), Cnr Airborne and Rosedale Roads, Albany,
Auckland 1310, New Zealand (a division of Pearson New Zealand Ltd)
Penguin Books (South Africa) (Pty) Ltd, 24 Sturdee Avenue,
Rosebank, Johannesburg 2196, South Africa

Penguin Books Ltd, Registered Offices:
80 Strand, London WC2R 0RL, England

Library of Congress Cataloging-in-Publication Data

Holabird, Katharine.
My first ballet class / written by Katharine Holabird ;
with illustrations by Helen Craig.
p. cm. — (Angelina Ballerina)
ISBN 978-0-448-44507-6 (hardcover with jacket)
1. Ballet—Juvenile literature. I. Craig, Helen, ill. II. Title.
GV1787.5.H64 2007
792.8—dc22
2006024544

10 9 8 7 6 5 4 3 2 1

Contents

I love to dance!   *4–5*

What to wear   *6–7*

Ready for class   *8–9*

Lesson time!   *10–11*

Warming up   *12–13*

Dancing together   *14–15*

Jump up high!   *16–17*

Dressing up   *18–19*

Telling a story   *20–21*

Famous ballets   *22–23*

Imagine!   *24–25*

Ballerina dreams   *26–27*

Show time!   *28–29*

A mouse ballet   *30–31*

Acknowledgments   *32*

I love to dance!

If you enjoy dancing then you'll love going to ballet classes. You'll learn lots of ballet steps and enjoy practicing them with your friends. Ballet class is so much fun—it's the best thing since cheddar cheese!

I just can't stop dancing!

Before you go

It's so exciting when you start ballet lessons. Every day you've been thinking about ballet and looking forward to dancing in your ballet slippers and leotard, and now the big day has finally arrived. You can't wait to put on your ballet clothes, point your toes, and dance!

I even dance in my dreams!

It's lots of fun to dance with your friends.

Meeting new friends

When you go to ballet class you'll meet lots of other young dancers. You can practice all the ballet positions together, and soon you won't feel shy at all!

Practice makes perfect!

At first the ballet positions may seem a bit strange, but don't worry. Your teacher will encourage you and show you how to get the positions right.

I put all my ballet things in a special bag.

What to wear

I love to go to ballet lessons—they're so much fun! I pack all the things I will need in my ballet bag. You don't have to bring much, just some ballet slippers to dance in and comfortable clothes to move around in.

Ready to dance

You'll need a stretchy leotard with a pair of tights and a twirly skirt. Don't forget your ballet slippers!

Pretty in pink

My favorite color is pink, but there are lots of other pretty colors you can choose from.

Star of the show

Ballerinas wear special
clothes for big performances.
This frilly skirt is called a
tutu and is made from lots
of layers of tulle.

This tutu feels
soft and bouncy!

Tutus look so pretty when you're twirling onstage!

Extra-special

Some costumes are decorated with
pretty beads or sequins, so they look
extra-special. The glittery butterflies on
this ballet dress will sparkle onstage!

Ready for class

The first thing you do when you arrive at ballet school is get changed. As soon as you put on your leotard, tights, and slippers, you'll be ready to start. It's a good idea to bring a hairbrush and some pretty hairbands so you can fix your hair.

Ballet friends help each other.

Ballet slippers

There are special ballet shops where you can buy your ballet slippers. When you try on a pair of slippers, make sure they are comfortable and that you have room to wiggle your toes!

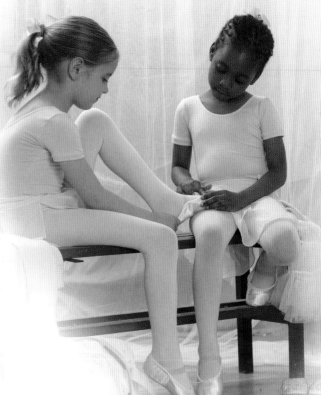

Looking neat

Dancers need to be neat and tidy. They tie back their hair so they can see properly. If you can't tie your own ribbons, ask a classmate to help.

Ballerinas
always tie
their ribbons
carefully so
they won't
trip.

I wear a pretty
ribbon in my hair.

Pointe shoes

Grown-up ballerinas have to look
neat and tidy, too. They wear ballet
slippers called "pointe" shoes that
are fastened with ribbons around
their ankles. The ribbons are tied
in a special way so that they look
neat and won't come undone.

Lesson time!

Ballet lessons take place in a big room called a studio, where there is lots of space for dancing. There are mirrors on the walls so you can check your ballet positions and a smooth wooden floor to dance on.

Miss Lilly is the best ballet teacher in all of Mouseland!

Music

In class you'll dance to lots of different types of music, sometimes fast and sometimes slow. There may be a pianist or you might dance to music from a tape or CD player.

Miss Quaver plays the piano in my ballet classes!

Stand in line!

At the start of every ballet lesson
the children line up in front of the
teacher while she does roll call. This
is so she can check who is present.
It's hard to wait patiently, but as
soon as your name is called you'll
be ready to dance.

The teacher is pleased to
see all the children.

Mouselings always warm up their tails!

Warming up

At the start of each class you should always warm up your muscles so you are ready to dance. Here are some fun stretching exercises to help you warm up. Remember to go slowly and really s-t-r-e-t-c-h!

Pitter-patter

Sit on the floor with your legs crossed. To warm up your hands, pretend it's raining and use your fingers to show raindrops falling down from the sky.

A growing seed

To warm up your arms, pretend you are a tiny seed that has been planted in the earth. Slowly lift your arms up in the air. As you stretch your arms way up high, imagine you are growing into a tall tree.

Remember to sit up straight like a real ballet dancer.

Good toes, naughty toes

Before you dance it's important to stretch the muscles in your legs and feet. Sit with your legs straight in front of you and point your feet. In my ballet class we call this "good toes" because you should always point your toes when you dance.

Now, flex your feet back the other way until your toes are pointing up to the ceiling. We call this "naughty toes!"

Point your toes!

Dancing together

One of the best things about going to ballet classes is dancing with your new friends. There are all kinds of fun steps you can try, but it can take a little while to get used to dancing with a partner or in a group.

Working together
In groups of three, these dancers listen to everyone's ideas before they decide on their dance routine.

I'm a little dancing seed!

Dancing flowers
They decide to be dancing flowers and pretend to grow from little seeds into big, beautiful flowers.

Teamwork
It takes good
teamwork to dance
well with others.
You need to think
about what your
friends are doing
as well as your
own routine!

Watch out!
The dancers carry
a delicate flower
garland as they
dance, so they must
watch one another
very carefully.

Dancing together is fun. Just remember to watch your partner and smile!

Jump up high!

I love to watch ballet dancers doing lots of exciting jumps and leaps—they look like they're as light as feathers! In ballet class you will learn some simple jumps at first, and with practice you'll soon be jumping for joy!

Jumping is lots of fun!

Jack-in-the-box

Pretend you are a jack-in-the-box ready to pop up. Be still and don't wiggle!

Jump as high as you can!

1. Start with your knees bent and your hands on the floor in front of you. Get ready to jump . . .

2. Imagine someone has taken the lid off the box. Push down into the floor as you spring up.

3. Jump way up with your back straight and your arms stretched up high. Remember to point your toes.

Can you jump in a pretty star shape?

Be a star!

To do a star jump, start with your knees bent and your hands on the floor. As you jump up open your legs wide and stretch your arms out to the side. Try to point your toes!

Dressing up

Wearing a costume when you dance is lots of fun and can really help you to get into character! In today's class the little dancers are all dressed up in special outfits. Can you guess what they are?

Be a butterfly

The children are pretending to be beautiful butterflies! They wear colorful tutus and sparkly wings. When they dance, they imagine they are flying around a lovely garden.

It's fun to dress up!

Listen to the music and soon you'll be flying!

Let's pretend
Gently raise and lower your arms in graceful movements and you'll feel just like a butterfly fluttering its wings.

Be delicate
Take little steps in time to the music, and be as delicate as a butterfly as you dance.

Telling a story

Ballet is a way of telling a story using dance instead of words. Ballet dancers use their faces and bodies when they perform so the audience understands what is happening in the story even though there are no words. It's magic!

I love to dress up and practice making faces!

In the mirror

Try using your face and body to tell a story. Practice making faces like these and see if your classmates can guess what you're trying to show.

Surprised
To show you are surprised, put your hands on your face and open your mouth wide!

Sad
To pretend you are sad, tilt your head down and look toward the ground.

Happy
Showing that you are happy is really easy! All you have to do is smile!

Love

To show "love" put both your hands upon your heart and look up. Try thinking about all the people you care about.

Sleep

To pretend you are sleepy, close your eyes and rest your head on your arms as if you are lying on a lovely, soft pillow.

I'm making a happy face!

Well done!

Famous ballets

Many wonderful stories have been transformed into exciting ballets. Some ballets like *Sleeping Beauty* and *Cinderella* are based on fairy tales that you probably know very well! Here are just a few of the famous ballets performed onstage all around the world.

Swan Lake
A beautiful princess called Odette is turned into a white swan by an evil wizard. A prince falls in love with her and tries to save her.

Sleeping Beauty
Princess Aurora pricks her finger on a spinning wheel and falls asleep under a magic spell. To wake up, she must be kissed by her true love.

What's your favorite ballet?

Cinderella

Cinderella's stepsisters won't let her go to the ball. Just when all hope is lost, her Fairy Godmother appears and makes her the belle of the ball!

Coppelia

Coppelia is a doll who looks so real that people think she's alive! Everyone falls in love with her, even the old toymaker!

Imagine!

When you dance, you can be anything you want to be—all you have to do is use your imagination. Sometimes during class, the teacher lets you create your own special dances.

Henry loves to make up his own dances.

Listen to the music

The music that's playing helps the class create their dance. As they listen to the music, they think about whether it is fast or slow, happy or sad. How does the music make them feel?

Galloping

The music reminds the class of the sound of horses' hooves and they decide to dance like little ponies. They trot across the room in time to the music.

Clip-clop, clip-clop!

We always enjoy making up dances together!

Prancing ponies
When the music slows
down, the children lift their legs up
high and prance like ponies. As the
music gets faster, they gallop and jump!

This is my favorite costume!

Ballerina dreams

Sometimes a real ballerina comes to class to tell you about being a dancer. It's exciting—especially if she brings a beautiful costume! This ballerina has been dancing for years, but once upon a time she was a beginner, too!

Costumes

Ballet costumes are so pretty and sparkly. Each costume is specially made by hand to fit the ballerina perfectly.

Decorations

This costume is decorated with lots of sequins and beads.

This is the prettiest tutu ever!

It takes time to become a ballerina, but with hard work your dreams could come true!

Perfect poise

The ballerina looks so elegant as she dances. She holds her head up high and keeps her back straight. Her arms and even her fingertips look graceful!

Fancy footwork

It's amazing to watch the ballerina dancing on the tips of her toes! This is called dancing "en pointe." The toes of her ballet shoes are made of layers of canvas and glue that make them hard enough to dance on!

She's like Serena Silvertail, my favorite dancer.

Miss Lilly helps us prepare for our shows.

Show time!

At the end of the year, many ballet schools put on a performance. It's a chance for young dancers to show people what they have learned. A performance takes lots of preparation and hard work, but it's exciting and lots of fun, too!

Dress rehearsals

A few days before the show, you have a dress rehearsal. This is when you all get dressed up in your costumes and practice your dance.

Practice makes perfect!

Makeup

Makeup helps the audience see your face as you dance. The dress rehearsal is the time to try out your makeup before the real show.

Get into character

You can also use makeup to create characters. You could be an animal, a clown, or even a wicked witch! With your makeup done and your costume on, you'll feel transformed!

What are these dancers going to be?

Here we go!

After the finishing touches are done, it's time to practice your routine one last time before the big day!

Don't be late for rehearsals, Henry!

A mouse ballet

When it's time for the show to begin, the music plays and the dancers wait behind the curtain. They are a little nervous at first, but they quickly begin to enjoy themselves. The dancers are being happy little mice—just like me and my friends!

Coming onstage
One by one the dancers tiptoe onstage as quiet as little mice!

Ready to go
The dancers have made mouse ears and tails! They even have whiskers and tiny noses like us!

On with the show!

Mouse ears

The mice stop to wash their ears before they set off to find some tasty cheese to eat.

Mouse paws

The ballerinas hold up their hands and pretend to have little paws. They enjoy dancing onstage with their mouseling friends.

See you next time!

Acknowledgments

We would like to thank the following for their help
in preparing and producing this book:

All the students of Central School of Ballet who attended the
photo shoot; Central School of Ballet for their kind permission to
photograph the book there; Maggie Purr who trained and graduated
from Central School of Ballet and now teaches there, for
her time, advice, and patience during the photo shoot.